Saying goodbye to...
A Grandparent

Chrysalis Children's Books

First published in the UK in 2003 by
Chrysalis Children's Books
64 Brewery Road
London N7 9NT

© Chrysalis Books Plc 2003
Illustrations © Chrysalis Books Plc 2003

Text by Nicola Edwards

A Belitha Book

Editorial manager: Joyce Bentley
Senior editor: Sarah Nunn
Project editor: Jean Coppendale
Designer: Clare Sleven
Illustrations by: Sarah Roper
Picture researcher: Jenny Barlow
Consultant: Jenni Thomas, Chief Executive
The Child Bereavement Trust

ISBN 184 138 8343

British Library Cataloguing in Publication
Data for this book is available from the
British Library.

Printed in China

Foreword

Confronting death and dying as an adult
is difficult but addressing these issues with
children is even harder. Children need to
hear the truth and sharing a book can
encourage and help both adults and
children to talk openly and honestly
about their feelings, something many of
us find difficult to do.

Written in a clear, sensitive and very
caring way, the **Saying Goodbye To...**
series will help parents, carers and
teachers to meet the needs of grieving
children. Reading about the variety of
real life situations, including the death of
a pet, may enable children to feel less
alone and more able to make sense of the
bewildering emotions and responses they
feel when someone dies.

Being alongside grieving children is not
easy, the **Saying Goodbye To...** series
will help make this challenging task a
little less daunting.

Jenni Thomas OBE
Chief Executive
The Child Bereavement Trust

The Child Bereavement Trust
Registered Charity No. 04049

All reasonable efforts have been made to trace the relevant copyright holders of the images contained
within this book. If we were unable to reach you, please contact Chrysalis Children's Books.

Cover Bubbles/Loisjoy Thurston 1 Bubbles/Clarissa Leahy 4 Bubbles/Loisjoy Thurston 5 Bubbles/Chris
Rout 6 Corbis/Tom Stewart 7 Corbis/Mug Shots 8 Bubbles/Denise Hager 9 Bubbles/Loisjoy Thurston 10
Bubbles/Clarissa Leahy 11 Getty Images/David Harry Stewart 12 Bubbles/Jennie Woodcock 13
Bubbles/Chris Rout 14 Bubbles/Peter Sylent 15 Bubbles/Angela Hampton 16 Corbis/Nathan Benn 17
Getty Images/Jean Louis Batt 18 Bubbles/Loisjoy Thurston 19 Bubbles/Angela Hampton 20 Corbis/Jon
Feingersh 21 Bubbles/Loisjoy Thurston 22 Corbis/David Turnley 23 Getty Images/Zigy Kaluzny 24
Corbis/Philip Gould 25 Photofusion/Paul Baldesere 26 Bubbles/Loisjoy Thurston 27 Bubbles/Angela
Hampton 28 Bubbles/Peter Sylent 29 Corbis/Tom & Dee Ann McCarthy.

Contents

Growing old

Children often feel very close to their grandparents. They can be an important part of their lives, and when they die children may feel terribly sad. Growing old is a natural part of life. People fall ill more often as they get older. Sometimes children visit and help grandparents who are unwell.

As people grow old, their bodies gradually wear out and stop working as well as they used to.

Something to think about...
At first it might upset you to see someone you care about looking unwell. But old people who are ill usually find it **comforting** to see their grandchildren and like to spend time with them.

Rosa liked to help her grandma.

What death means

When someone dies their body stops working and cannot be mended. Breathing stops, the heart stops beating and the brain doesn't work any more. A dead person can't feel afraid or be in pain. It can be hard for children to believe that they won't see their grandparent again. This may make them feel very sad.

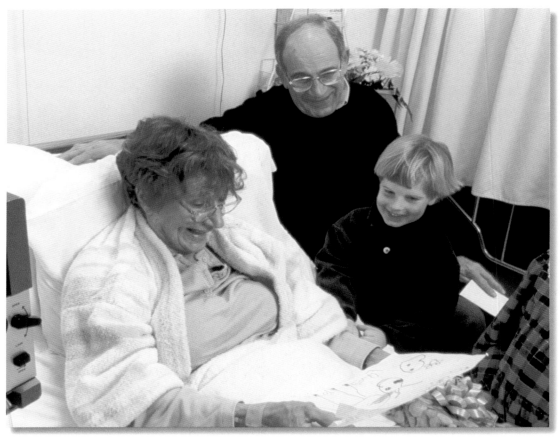

When Jake's nanny was dying he visited her at the **hospice**. He was glad his nan was in a peaceful place with kind people to look after her.

Cara cried when
her mum told her
that her grandad
had died.

Something to think about...
It's natural to want to ask lots of questions about
what has happened when someone dies.

Part of the family

Some children see their grandparents often and get to know them well. Sometimes grandparents live in the same house as the rest of the family. If they become ill, the children may help to look after them. The old people may be ill for a long time.

Grandparents are an important part of many families.

Something to think about...
When someone dies after a long illness, it's natural to have lots of different feelings and even feel **relieved** that the person is not suffering anymore

Some grandparents help to look after their grandchildren while the parents are out at work.

Far away from home

Some children don't see their grandparents very much. Their grandparents may live too far away for them to visit very often – perhaps they live even in a different country.

Jane and Matt's grandma taught them all about the different flowers in her garden when they saw in her.

Children who don't know their grandparents well sometimes don't feel sad when they die. They may worry because they think they ought to feel sad. But there is no right or wrong way to feel when someone dies.

Alan loved spending time talking with his grandad. His grandad always had lots of stories to tell him.

A special relationship

Grandparents often like giving their grandchildren special treats, or taking them for days out. They may let their grandchildren do things that their parents wouldn't allow them to do. They may tell them off less, too! When the old people die their grandchildren may feel very sad because they know how much they'll miss them.

Anya's grandparents loved taking her on trips to the seaside.

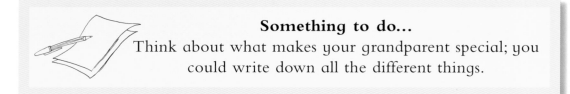

Something to do...
Think about what makes your grandparent special; you could write down all the different things.

12

Rosa felt that she could tell her grandma anything.

It's not fair!

Children who are **grieving** can have lots of confusing feelings when their grandparents die. They may think it's unfair that their friends' grandparents are still alive.

When Danny's nanny died he was cross with his little brother. He was too young to understand what had happened.

They may be cross that life just carries on normally for everyone else. Some children may even feel angry with their grandparent for dying and leaving them to feel so sad. These are natural ways to feel when someone dies.

Gina was glad her grandmother had taught her how to draw. It would always remind her of her gran.

Something to think about...
If you are feeling angry because your grandparent has died it can help if you share your feelings with someone you **trust**.

15

Feeling sad

Children can feel terribly sad and lost when their grandparent dies. They find it hard to understand that they will never see them again. Some children feel like crying when they are sad. Crying can be a good way of letting sad feelings out. But other children can feel just as sad without crying.

Mark cried when he thought about how much he missed his grandma.

Something to think about...
Sharing feelings of grief with other people can help everyone to comfort each other.

16

Saying goodbye to a grandparent

When Rachel's grandpa died she could see that her mum was very upset because he had been her daddy. Rachel was worried about her mum. She gave her mum a big hug.

Asking questions

When someone dies it's natural for children to want to ask questions to help them understand what has happened. Sometimes adults try to **protect** children by not talking about what has happened. They worry that explaining things to children might upset them. Children may try to protect their parents, too. They may not ask questions in case it upsets their mum and dad. But being left out can just make children feel more confused and worried.

People told Tim his grandad had gone to 'a better place'. Tim didn't understand what they meant. He wondered whether it was a place he could visit.

Ling's dad helped her when her grandmother died by answering all her questions.

Something to think about...
If you are worried about anything tell someone you trust about your feelings. They'll talk to you about your questions, even if they don't have all the answers.

Helping each other

When an old person dies they may leave behind their husband or wife, their children and their grandchildren. This means that many people can be left feeling sad and lonely. Families who are **mourning** can help each other during this very sad time. This could be by doing something practical, such as helping out with the shopping, or just by being around to listen when someone feels like talking.

David's mum gave him his grandfather's watch. It would always remind him of his grandad.

> **Something to do...**
> Think about what you could do to help a grandparent who has been **bereaved**. You could spend time with them, help with the garden, go for walks or look at old family photographs together.

Lucy and her grandma talked together for a long time when Lucy's grandpa died. It helped both of them.

Preparing for a funeral

A **funeral** is a special service in which people come together to remember the person who has died. The dead body is brought to the funeral in a **coffin**. Some funerals are **religious**, others are not, because different people have different beliefs. Children need to know what will happen at the funeral so that they can decide whether or not they would like to go to it.

Luke helped to choose the flowers for his gran's funeral.

Sara chose a hymn
for the choir
to sing at her
grandad's funeral.

Something to think about...
If you decide not to go to your grandparent's funeral,
you could still take part by helping to get things
ready for it. You could help choose some flowers or
write some special words or a prayer.

23

Saying goodbye

At a funeral people who cared about the person who has died, show their **respect** for them and say goodbye. It can be difficult for children to see the people they love looking upset and crying. But it's natural to feel sad at a funeral and people are there to comfort each other.

Laura sat with her mum at her grandpa's funeral service. She was pleased to be there with her family to say goodbye.

A funeral gives people a chance to share their memories of the person who has died.

Something to do...
You might decide to take part in the funeral in some way, for example, by helping people to find their seats or lighting a candle during the service. It's up to you.

Sharing memories

When an old person dies, lots of people in the family are affected by their death and have their own memories to share. Families may feel particularly sad on special days, such as at Christmas, **Diwali** or **Hanukah**.

Looking at photos helped Jade to remember the happy times she'd spent with her nanny.

At these times there may be lots of reminders that the person isn't around any more. But people can talk about the person who died and remember some of the things that they did together.

Fiona helped to look after her grandad's **allotment**.

Something to do...
Think about what you could do to help you remember your grandparent. All your memories are like gifts you will always have from your grandparent.

Part of your life

It can take time to feel happy again after someone you love has died. Grieving is natural and you can't hurry it. After a while your memories of the person who died will not feel as sad. It can also help children when they think that their grandparent was able to enjoy a long life.

Jonathan was glad he'd known his grandad. He felt lucky because he knew that not all children have grandparents.

Something to think about...
Sharing memories can help people to comfort each other and feel happier during sad times. It's natural to feel both happy and sad when you're grieving.

Nina's family often used her grandma's favourite pot at meal times. It helped everyone to remember her.

Glossary

allotment   a small piece of rented land used for growing vegetables, fruit or flowers

bereaved   being left behind when someone you love or care about dies

coffin   the container in which a dead body is placed

comforting   helping someone who is sad to feel better

Diwali   an important festival in the Hindu religion

funeral   a special service in which people remember a person who has died and say goodbye to them

grieving   the natural process of feeling sad after someone has died

guilty   feeling bad, as if it's your fault that something is wrong

Hanukah   the Jewish festival of light

hospice   a building where people who are dying are looked after

mourning   the ways in which people who have been bereaved show their feelings of grief

mosque   a holy building where Muslims worship

protect   taking care of someone, keeping them from harm

relief   to feel happier after a difficult time

religious   to do with a belief in God

respect   a polite attitude or manner which shows that someone is thought well of

trust   feeling that someone will not let you down

Useful addresses

The Child Bereavement Trust
A charity offering training, resources and support for professional carers and teachers working with bereaved children and grieving adults
Aston House
High Street
West Wycombe
Bucks HP14 3AG
Tel: 01494 446648
Information and Support Line: 0845 357 1000
E-mail: enquiries@childbereavement.org.uk
Website: www.childbereavement.org.uk
★ New interactive website where children and adults can send emails

Childhood Bereavement Network
An organization offering bereaved children and their families and caregivers information about the support services available to them.
Huntingdon House
278-290 Huntingdon Street
Nottingham NG1 3LY
Tel: 0115 911 8070
E-mail: cbn@ncb.org.uk
Website: www.ncb.org.uk/cbn

ChildLine
Childline's free, 24-hour helpline is staffed by trained counsellors, offering help and support to children and young people. The website includes information on bereavement.
Freepost 1111
London N1 0BR
Tel: 0800 11 11 (Freephone 24 hours)
Website: www.childline.org.uk

Cruse Bereavement Care
The Cruse helpline offers information and counselling to people of all ages who have been bereaved. The website offers additional information and support.

Cruse House
126 Sheen Road
Richmond
Surrey TW9 1UR
Tel: 020 8322 7227
Helpline: 0870 167 1677 (Mondays to Fridays 9.30am–5pm)
Website: www.crusebereavementcare.org.uk

The Samaritans
An organization offering support and help to anyone who is emotionally distressed.
Tel: 08457 90 90 90 (24 hours)
Website: www.samaritans.org.uk

Winston's Wish
A charity offering support and information to bereaved children and their families.
The Clara Burgess Centre
Gloucestershire Royal Hospital
Great Western Road
Gloucester GL1 3NN
Tel: 01452 394377
Family Line: 0845 20 30 40 5 (Mondays to Fridays 9.30am–5pm)
E-mail: info@winstonswish.org.uk
Website: www.winstonswish.org

Youth Access
An organization providing information about youth counselling services.
1-2 Taylors Yard
67 Alderbrook Road
London SW12 8AD
Tel: 020 8772 9900 (Monday to Fridays 9am–1pm, 2-5pm)
E-mail: admin@youthaccess.org.uk

Index